Disney's

My Very First Dictionary

Disney's

My Very

Abradale Press

Harry N. Abrams, Inc.,

Publishers

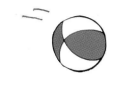

First Dictionary

by Vincent Jefferds

Project Director: Darlene Geis

Designer: Leane Brenes

The Library of Congress has cataloged the Abrams edition as follows:

Jefferds, Vincent H.
   Disney's my very first dictionary / by Vincent Jefferds.
     p. cm.
   Summary: Provides illustrated definitions for 476 words.
   ISBN 0–8109–1146–9
   1. English language—Dictionaries, Juvenile. [1. English
language—Dictionaries.] I. Walt Disney Productions. II. Title.
III. Title: My very first dictionary.
PE1628.5.J44 1989
423'.1—dc19   88–24135
Abradale ISBN 0–8109–8180–7

Printed and bound in Hong Kong

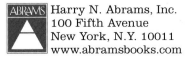 Harry N. Abrams, Inc.
100 Fifth Avenue
New York, N.Y. 10011
www.abramsbooks.com

The selection of basic words for this dictionary

was made in consultation with members of

the staff of the famous Little Red School House in

New York City.

A Note to Parents

Enjoy this book! Snuggle up with your child and spend a few minutes laughing and talking over Vincent Jefferds's thoughtful, humorously rhymed meanings of words with their Disney illustrations. Notice how the pictures relate to the printed words. Give your child a chance to ask questions. These questions help youngsters understand the ideas and the humor of the book.

After reading a letter section—the "A"s, for example—you and your child might try to think of other words that begin with "A." You help your child learn to read every time you sit down to read together. You also help your child *want* to read whenever *you* read the newspaper, a magazine, a book (including the phone book!), your mail. Your children see that reading is important to their parents. They will want to be readers just like you. A dictionary of their very own is an important step toward that goal.

So . . . read your favorite definitions, or the whole book, again and again and enjoy it. We did!

Elizabeth Servidio
Kathleen McCullagh
First Grade Teachers
The Little Red School House
New York City

Aa

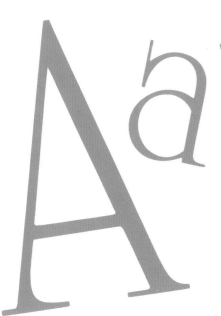

accident

When something bad
   or something grand
Happens without
   being planned.
Here's an accident
   you can see—
Goofy flew
   into a tree!

add

If you put things together they make more,
Like two and two add up to four.

address

On a letter to you, the writer will give
The street number and town in which you live.

adventure

It could be on a boat or in a zoo,
An exciting thing that happens to you.

afraid

When you think you
   might be hurt,
The fear you feel
   makes you alert.
See Mickey running
   from a bear;
He runs much faster
   when there's a scare.

afternoon

From noon to dusk
   you play and run;
But when you see
   the setting sun,
That's the end of
   the afternoon.
It all seems over
   much too soon.

age

If someone asks you,
   "What's your age?"
The answer that
   you give
Will be a number
   that will show
How many years
   you've lived.

air

There is something nice about the air.
You can't see it, but it's always there.
Take a breath . . . and then again.
The air gives you good oxygen.

airplane

I could try, but I can't fly,
I'd just fall to the ground.
But big and heavy airplanes
Fly past the speed of sound.

airport

Everybody needs a home;
Nothing does well all alone.
The airport's where the airplane can
Land, and rest, and fly again.

alone

It's nice to be with all your friends,
And laugh and talk and play,
But there are times to be alone,
When you haven't much to say.
Perhaps you'd rather stay at home
And think and read that day.

alphabet

The letters
    form a family
That runs from
    good old A to Z.

ambulance

If you're very sick,
    there's a special car
To take you from
    the place you are,
And, whether you
    are big or small,
It gets you quickly
    to the hospital.

angry

Look at Donald, all upset.
Hear him shout and yell. And yet
His anger passes in a while,
And once again we'll see his smile.

animal

A living creature that can move;
As it grows up, its skills improve.

ant

What piles of food
    he can collect,
For a tiny
    six-legged insect!

ape

If you call him monkey,
    then you fail:
Unlike a monkey,
    he has no tail.
But if he's not
    as fast a starter,
He makes it up
    by being smarter.

apple

"An apple a day keeps the doctor away,"
My parrot used to scream.
A nice round fruit that's good for you
Is really what we mean.
They come in red and green and yellow;
Eat them when they're ripe and mellow.

apron

An apron, as your
    mother knows,
Keeps splash and
    splatter from
Your clothes.

aquarium

Colorful fish from
    some far-off sea
Live in tanks of
    water for us to see.
The fish never make
    a noise or a fuss,
They get such a kick
    out of watching us.

artist

It took an artist
    to paint and draw
The cat and fish
    that you just saw.

ask

If you don't know how to get it done,
Try to get the answer from someone.

asleep

When you're asleep
    you're not awake,
Which gives your
    busy Mom a break.

11

astronaut
A brave flier
  who makes a trip
Far into space
  in a spaceship.

Bb

baby
A child who is very very young
And often yells at the top of its lungs.

bad
The opposite
  of good is bad.
If you are bad
  it makes folks mad.

bake
Many of the foods we eat
We cook in ovens with dry heat.

ball
Something round and made for fun.
It can bounce and roll and run.
But it will lay around all day
Unless you throw it and make it play.

balloon
A rubber toy filled with gas or air—
You can buy one almost anywhere.

12

banana

A long thin fruit in yellow seal,
It's fun to eat and fun to peel.

bandage

In this picture,
   as you can see,
Goofy is binding
   up a tree.

bank

If you have some cash to spare,
Find a bank and leave it there.
The bank will keep it safe and sound
Until your need for it comes round.

barn

A kind of building
   farmers need
To house the animals
   and their feed.

basket

Goofy carried a snake named Randall
In a hamper with a handle.
When it got chilly in the fall,
That darn snake refused to crawl.

bat

It's easy to swing this wooden stick,
But hitting the ball is quite a trick.

bath

An all-over wash
  you take in a tub
To get off the dirt;
  use soap and rub.

beach

Sand and pebbles near the sea;
That's where I would like to be.

bear

A wild animal, large and furry;
If you meet one, leave in a hurry.

bed

A place to sleep
  that is the best,
With a pillow where
  my head can rest,
And there's a
  blanket just for me.
How can a cat
  sleep in a tree?

bedroom

Remember what has
  just been said?
The bedroom's where
  you keep your bed.

bee
You had better show respect
For this little flying insect.
He's a cute and fuzzy thing,
But he has a nasty sting.

belt
Around your waist you wrap this thing
Made of leather, cloth, or string.

bicycle
Oh, my! How
　good it feels
To ride along
　on a pair of wheels.

big
Large and thick,
　and that's not all;
Whatever it is,
　it's also tall.

bird
Two legs, a beak,
　and feathered wings;
It flies through the air.
　It sometimes sings.

birthday
This is the day you
　arrived on earth;
We celebrate the
　day of your birth.

15

bite

To take from something
    a small piece,
By pressing firmly
    with your teeth.

blackboard

White chalk shows best upon the black;
Teacher won't like it when she comes back!

blanket

A warm cover on the bed.
Mine is squares of black and red.

boat

When you sail in the
    water for a ride,
This is what
    you sit inside.

bones

Hard parts in your body
    that keep it in shape.
Without all the bones,
    your body would drape.

book

Paper pages between
   a cover
Bring great joy
   to a book lover.
Of all the things that
   one might mention,
Books may be the
   best invention.

boots

In rough and
   muddy water,
Boots are hard
   to beat;
They cover a part
   of both your legs,
As well as both
   your feet.

bottle

You pour the liquid
   from its top,
And stand it up when
   you want to stop.
If you pour like
   the Mad Hatter,
You will only
   splash and splatter.

box

It has four straight sides, and the top is handy;
It can hold toys, or clothes, or candy.

boy

Nothing is more
   certain than
A boy child grows
   to be a man.

branch

This is a live piece
of wood, you see.
It is the arm of
a growing tree.

brave

If you are brave you
must be prepared
Not to run from danger
when you're scared.

bread

This is a food made
mostly of flour,
Put in the oven and
baked for an hour.

breakfast

I've heard a number
of people say
It's the first and best
meal of the day.

brick

Pieces of clay baked hard and rough
Will make a house that's strong and tough.

bridge

It can be built of wood,
 steel, or concrete.
For crossing rivers and roads,
 a bridge can't be beat.

broom

A brush on a handle. You
 know what it's for—
For cleaning the steps,
 and sweeping the floor.
But at night, it's
 best to hide them.
Some people think
 that witches ride them.

brother

If a boy in your family has the
same dad and mother,
Then the boy that we speak
of is your very own brother.

brush

A bunch of hairs upon a holder
Is what we call a brush.
But the list would fill a folder,
If we didn't have to rush.
There's a brush for painting, a brush for clothes,
And one for ladies' hair, lord knows.
A brush for teeth, a brush for the floor,
A brush for pets, and many more.

bubble

Fill a glass for son or daughter,
Blow some bubbles in the soapy water.
Each little ball of air will pop
After it rises to the top.

build

Busy in sunny and
rainy weather,
Mr. Eagle is putting
a house together.

bus

An enormous
motorcar
That will take
you near or far.
It carries lots
of folks inside.
You usually have
to pay to ride.

Cc

button

This thing is round, everyone knows,
And used for fastening our clothes.
It slips right through a slitted hole
And helps keep out the wind and cold.

cake

Made of eggs and sugar and flour,
Baked in the oven about an hour.
And when it's done, it would be nice
To offer some good friend a slice.

camera

A wonderful box for you and me
That lets us take photos of things we see.
Donald is angry as he can be.
He wanted a picture of this tree.

candle

A column of wax with a string through the middle,
It poses something of a riddle.
If you don't light it, it lasts all day;
If you do light it, it melts away.

car

I am sure that
   you've already been
Riding in this
   four-wheeled machine.
It has an engine
   to make it run.
When you can drive,
   it will be fun.

carpenter

The carpenter
   is very good;
He's trained to make
   things out of wood.
With pen and paper
   I write a poem;
With hammer and saw
   he makes a home.

castle

A very old building,
With walls thick and stout,
To give shelter to friends
And keep enemies out.

cat

A furry pet that
is very nice,
And keeps the house
quite free of mice.

caterpillar

He's something like
   a short, fat worm;
If you touch him,
   he will squirm.
I admit I don't
   know why
He turns into
   a butterfly.

21

cave

A big hole in a hill
  or a pile of rocks.
It might make a den
  for a wolf or a fox,
But hundreds of years
  ago there were times when
It was a home for
  the shaggy cavemen.

ceiling

It is the top
  part of a room.
You have to clean
  it with a broom.
Did you ever
  get the feeling
You'd like to walk
  upon the ceiling?
I have, and I'll
  tell you why—
I'd like to
  imitate a fly.

chair

A seat with a back
  that one can sit in;
It might hold two if
  they are both thin.

cheese

A food that's soft and smooth as silk,
And it is made from wholesome milk.

chicken

This is the word
  that you use when
A chick becomes a
  nice young hen.

child

A youngster who gives
    parents lots of joy,
Whether it's a
    girl or boy.

chimney

You build a chimney
    that's fireproof,
Running from fireplace
    through the roof,
So it can carry
    out the smoke.
If it didn't,
    you would choke.

chocolate

A sweet brown food to eat or drink,
It's made from cocoa beans, I think.
Making chocolate can be fun.
Here is Donald stirring some.

circle

A ring that is perfectly round.
Lots of examples can be found;
A bike wheel is one good thing
That has the shape of this round ring.

circus

Where animals do
    clever things
And acrobats take
    wing on rings;
Where clowns get
    in a silly fix
While they're performing
    funny tricks.

city

Your first trip there
    will pop your eyes.
It's a town of
    the biggest size.

OUR HERO

23

classroom

A room in school
  where children go
To make their fund
  of knowledge grow.

clean

I swept the dirt off
  the kitchen floor
So it's not dirty
  any more.
Would it be nice,
  or would it be mean,
To try to sweep a
  fat eel clean?

climb

To move upward with foot and hand,
On a ladder or some steep land.

clock

This machine ticks (some even chime).
In any case, it tells the time.

clothes

These are all the things you wear,
Like coats and hats and underwear.

cloud

A lot of water drops passing by,
Floating together in the sky.

cold

When it is cold, what you have got
Is just the opposite of hot,
Like winter when the cold winds blow,
And you have lots of ice and snow.

color

Some of the colors
    you have seen
Are red, and yellow,
    blue, and green.

comb

If you want to make
    your hair look neat,
A comb is a tool
    that can't be beat.

cook

It's what you do when
    you give food some heat
When preparing it
    for friends to eat.

corner

Remember Little
   Jack Horner
Eating a pie
   in the corner?
But this word is not
   about something to eat.
It's where two walls
   or two roads meet.

cow

This animal is a
   mother's dream;
It gives the children
   milk and cream.

cradle

This is a baby's
   legless bed
That is built to stand
   on rockers instead.

crash

When something breaks
   with a loud noise,
We all come running,
   girls and boys.
Goofy's rocket fell
   back to the ground
And landed with
   an awful sound.

crayon

I can use these colored sticks
To draw a cow or house of bricks.
Wax and chalk, they both work fine,
Making drawings or a sign.

crowd

A large part of the human race,
Packed together in one place.

crown

If you are a queen or king,
You rule over everything.
You wear a kind of gold headdress,
Which can make your hair an awful mess.

cry

When you're sad
  it's no surprise
If some tears fall
  from your eyes.

cup

A bowl of coffee you can sip,
Holding its handle in your grip.
This owner's ready to close up,
But Goofy wants another cup.

curtain

Cloth cut to cover a window,
Some hang high, some hang low.
If hung too low, you may find one
Hanging in the aquarium.

27

daisy
A small white flower
growing wild,
With a yellow center,
simply styled.

dance
To move your feet
  'round and 'round
In time to the
  music's happy sound.

dangerous
When I see things
  not safe for me,
I know enough to
  leave them be.

dark
When you have so little light,
You can't rely upon your sight,
Like when the sun has set at night.

daughter
No matter how old she may be,
She's a girl in the family.

day
This is all the time you get
Between sunrise and sunset.

deep
Going down for a long distance,
The way a diver does, for instance.

deer
A beast who does on plant life feed,
Its one defense is its great speed.

dentist
Your kindly dentist is always there
To give your teeth the best of care.

desert
"What good is land,
  if it's all sand?"
I asked my
  little daughter.
"For things to grow,
  I'm sure you know,
To sand you
  must add water."

dictionary
A book that tells
  you what words mean;
You can look up
  cat or submarine.

dig
To make a hole to
  build a home,
Or make a hole to
  hide your bone.

dinosaur

A giant reptile; some lived on plants,
And some grew as big as three elephants.

dirty

We can say as a general rule,
You are clean when you leave for school;
But "dirty" is what mom is saying
When you return from outdoor playing.

dish

A shallow bowl from
    which we eat,
It helps to keep our
    dinner neat.
Doc cleaned his plate
    of all the food;
He was in a
    hungry mood.

doctor

A person whom we go to see.
He looks us over carefully,
He gives us good advice, and then
He cures us with his medicine.

dog

A four-legged mammal covered with hair,
You will see him everywhere.
A dog has one great claim to fame—
Of all the beasts, he is most tame.

doll

In any toy store you can see
Toys that look like a real baby;
You will also see, now and then,
Playthings that look like girls and men.

door

I will tell you what a door's about:
It can let you in or let you out
Of buildings, rooms, or anything
And has a hinge on which to swing.

double

Whether it's much or a small bit,
Double is twice as much of it.
An example I can give you
Is that four is double two.

draw

You take a piece of
    paper, and then
You make a picture
    with pencil or pen.

dragon

An animal that's make-believe
In many fairy tales.
It has bad breath and breathes out flames,
It's covered with green scales.
Its ugly feet have long, sharp claws;
Let's clip its sharp toenails.

drive

To make something
    move along.
In this case, something
    has gone wrong.

31

drum

Here's a loud
  musical trick:
Just beat on a drum
  with a short stick.
It makes a noisy
  boom! boom! boom!
And also makes folks
  leave the room.

dry

It's the least moisture
  you can get.
It's dry when it's not
  the least bit wet.

duck

This large bird goes swimming around;
He prefers water to the ground.

Ee

early

If both teams are playing well,
Which one will win is hard to tell.
It's too early to tell who's winning.
Early means near the beginning.

earth

One meaning that
  we can give
Is, "the planet on
  which we live."
Another with a
  different slant
Is, "the ground in
  which we plant."

eat

Put food in your mouth
    and chew a bit,
And after that you
    swallow it.

egg

A new life is sheltered
    inside a rounded shell.
It's what is laid by birds—
    and snakes, as well.

elephant

Look at him, so
    big and grand,
The largest animal
    on land.
He doesn't sing,
    he doesn't dance,
His wrinkled skin looks
    like unpressed pants.

end

The finish of something you began;
The last word of a story (like *Peter Pan*).

engine

A machine that turns energy into motion,
In cars on the road or ships on the ocean.
In other words, it makes them go
Forward or backward, fast or slow.

33

evening
When the sun's no longer bright,
Between afternoon and night.

exercise
Training of a special kind
For your body or your mind.

fairy
A small make-believe person,
    often with wings,
Who can do all kinds
    of magical things.

family
A group that loves one another:
Father, children, and their mother.

fan
On hot days we say a grateful prayer
For this machine that cools the air.

farm
A place where animals
   are grown,
And vegetable
   seeds are sown.

farmer
A man who looks
   after a farm
And stacks the hay
   up in his barn.

fast
A railway train is quick and fast.
In a race, Donald comes in last.

father
A man is called
   a father when
He has one child
   or several children.

feather
Here's a red plume to catch your eye.
A bird's coat of feathers helps it fly,
And also keeps the bird warm and dry.

find

To discover something
  you are looking for,
Like a butterfly
  or a secret door.

finish

To get to the end of a
  book you're reading,
Or complete a garden
  you've been weeding.

fire

Something that's burning, orange bright,
Gives off heat as well as light.
Goofy should have left more space
Between his books and the fireplace.

fireman

A brave man who runs about
Putting all the fires out.

fireworks

They announce their
  presence noisily,
And burn in bright
  colors for all to see.

36

first

If you are there when it's just begun,
Or if you are rated number one.

fish

I walked by the lake with my son and daughter
And watched the fish swim underwater.
If you took one out in the open air,
He would soon die if you kept him there.
This big blue fish has had to stop
For a starfish who is playing cop.

flag

A flag is a cloth to
 wave up above.
It stands for the country
 that you love.
Scrooge McDuck's
 flag is a honey—
It shows how much that
 duck loves money.

floor

The part of a room
 on which you walk,
Or you can sit on
 it and talk;
The part of the room
 where you put your feet
(Without it no room
 would be complete).
In fact, if a room
 had no floor at all,
When you opened the door,
 you'd take a fall.

flower

The colored parts of a plant that may
Make a very pretty bouquet.

fly

To move through the air
   without touching the ground.
This cow in the sky must
   be fooling around.

food

The things you eat
   to keep you well:
A list too long
   for me to tell.

forest

A big piece of
   land wherever
Lots of trees grow
   close together.

fox

A wild animal on
   the trail,
Where you might
   spot his bushy tail.

freeze

When cold makes things hard, just as if
All the water has become stiff.
In the Far North it's very nice:
You can build a house of ice.

friend

If it's a person you like a lot,
I guess a friend is what you've got.

frog

A small animal who lives
in ponds and streams,
And can jump beyond
your wildest dreams.
In storybooks they
sometimes are
Able to play
a big guitar.

fruit

From bush or tree, this tasty treat
Is the best part, which you can eat.

FETCH

fun

It's when you're having
a good time,
And what you're doing
suits you fine.

fur

I like animal hair
very much,
It's pretty and warm
and soft to touch.

garden

Here's Mickey working with a hoe,
To make his vegetables grow.
It's a place where you can spend hours
Also planting fruit and flowers.

gift

A present that is given to you.
Here is Donald giving one, too.

39

girl
She's a child playing
in her room.
She'll grow into
a woman soon.

glass
A hard material you can
see right through
Makes drinking glasses
and eyeglasses, too.

glue
Whether it's wood or
paper or leather,
This strong paste
sticks them together.

goldfish
A small golden fish you can easily get,
And keep in a tank as your very own pet.

good
Good people don't have to think twice,
They mostly do what's right and nice.

goose
It looks like a chick, by heck!
But it's larger, and has a longer neck.

grow
If you plant berries in a row,
They will get bigger, as you know.
In other words, they are going to grow.

guitar

Wherever you are,
   you're not far
From the sound
   of the guitar,
A musical instrument
   you can see
Played by the
   singers on TV.

hair

It grows straight or
   curly on your head;
Without it you'd be
   bald instead.

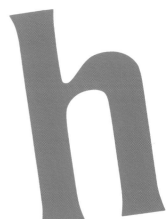

hammer

A heavy tool that you can take
To hit a nail or pound a stake.
Poor Goofy just did something dumb—
He missed the nail and hit his thumb.

handle

The part you hold,
   on pot or cup,
Made for your hand
   to pick it up.

hang

To place a jacket
   or a gown
On something so it
   won't fall down.

happy

So full of joy and
    merry feeling,
You feel like jumping
    through the ceiling.

hard

Look for a stone in
    your backyard.
A stone's not soft;
    a stone is hard.

hat

A special covering
    for your head,
To wear outdoors,
    and not in bed.

heavy

An iron bank that's hard to lift,
I wouldn't want even as a gift.
I couldn't lift it from the ground,
But Scrooge likes to carry money around.

helicopter

A plane that can fly straight ahead,
Or fly straight up and down instead.

help

You make a job easier for someone,
Like giving Dad a hand mowing the lawn.

hide

Sometimes I would
    like to be
Where nobody
    could look at me.
Sometimes I even
    hide my bat
So no one knows
    just where it's at.

high

A long way up is what's called high,
Like a mountain against the sky,
Or where a speedy hawk can fly.

hold

To have something in
    your arms or hands;
I don't think the
    turtle understands.

hole

Something you dig
    or tear into
When you make an
    opening in or through.

holiday

A holiday means no work or school;
Let's thank whoever made the rule.

home

If you live in far-off Rome,
That's the place that you call home.

honey

Something sweet to eat that's made by bees.
Don't chase the bees, if you please.

horse
This animal is
    remembered best
Ridden by cowboys
    in the West.

hospital
A place that you
    should get to quick
With somebody who's
    hurt or sick;
They have lots
    of doctors there,
And nurses who
    will give good care.

hot
If you're somewhere where it is *hot*.
It's the very, very warmest spot.

Ii

house
Whether it's a cottage or a roadside inn,
It's a building that people can live in.

ice cream
Made with milk and sugar
    and served cold,
It's a tasty treat
    for young and old.

Jj

jacket
A short coat for women and men,
And worn by children now and then.

44

jam
Mix fruit and sugar. Then the trick
Is to cook it till it's soft and thick.

jeans
Pants of denim,
   strong and tough,
Worn quite tight,
   without a cuff.

joy
When you feel so happy you could dance,
And leap and jump and hop and prance,
It's the glad feeling that fills you up
When at last you find your little lost pup.

juice
A liquid from plants. Whatever suits
Your taste, in vegetables or fruits.

jump
I'm sure by now that you have found
How to push your body off the ground.
If your legs are a sturdy pair,
They can push you right up in the air.

K

kettle
When you invite friends
   to come for tea,
Boil water in your kettle
   for the tea party.

45

key

A hard piece of metal to open a lock,
To be carried in a purse or sock.
If your father loses it, he decides fast
That mother must have had it last.

kick

You can use your foot to kick a ball,
But you never kick friends or pets at all.

kiss

It's more fun than
   riding a bike,
Touching lips with
   someone you like.

kitchen

If you're in a
   hungry mood,
This is where you
   look for food.

kite

A toy that's made of paper or cloth
And flies about the sky like a moth.
Amos is holding Ben Franklin's key.
He will learn about electricity!

knock

Monstro the whale is such a clown!
Here he's knocking Mickey down.
Even in fun it goes to show
What happens when you strike a blow.

ladder

Steps of wood or metal you can climb,
If you need to paint the house sometime.

lake

A body of water surrounded by land:
For swimming and boating it is grand.

lamp

When it's dark and
we can't see
This gives off light
for you and me.

land

The part of earth
not under water.
If you guessed right,
you get a quarter.

late

If you get there late that's not too good;
You got there after you said you would.

laugh

The sound you make when
something is funny,
And you cannot stop, for love
or money.

leaf
Part of the tree that's
flat and green.
When leaves fall to the
ground, Mickey rakes it clean.

learn
To get to know about something,
Like how and why a bee will sting.
This monkey wasn't taught a single thing.

lemonade
Sour lemon juice could spoil my day,
But with water and sugar it tastes OK.

letter
You write it and mail it
in an envelope.
The mailman has the
right address, I hope.

library
A place with lots of books to read,
Which you can borrow at your need.

light
It shines in the dark
For you and me,
Making it easy
For us to see.

listen
All day long sounds
    pour into your ear.
Listening is when
    you *try* to hear.

lock
What a lock is
    all about
Is to fasten doors
    to keep folks out.

look
When you use your
    eyes to see,
Like these folks
    looking at TV.

loud
When they practice, the little dears
Make so much noise, we hold our ears.

love
Goofy is kneeling on the floor
To someone he has a great liking for.

Mm

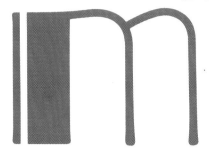

machine
Made mostly of metal,
with moving parts,
Push a switch or button
and it starts.

magic
Tricks that fool the eye and ear,
Like making a rabbit disappear.

magnet
A piece of metal that pulls other metals to it.
It's a good trick to try; you can easily do it.

mail
You and your family often get flocks
Of letters and packages in the mailbox.

man
A human being or a male.
He is not furry, he has no tail.
He's king of all the other creatures
And stands erect. He has nice features.

many
This is a word that means "a lot."
That's bad if it is bees you've got.

mask

A cover for the face
    can be fun,
But I'd be scared if
    I saw this one.

meat

For most of us,
    meat is a treat.
It's the part of
    animals we eat
After we've cooked it,
    sometimes at high heat.

medicine

It can be a liquid
    or a pill;
You take it to cure
    you from some ill.

metal

Hard material like
    steel and iron.
It's in the cars and
    planes we ride on.

milk

This is a liquid, white and wet;
If you milk a cow, that's what you get.
Something that you kids should know—
It will help your bones to grow.

minute

This is a little
   length of time,
Sixty seconds on
   the clock.
Time it while you
   read this rhyme
With other children
   on the block.

mirror

A piece of glass
   where you see yourself,
Exactly as
   you look.
But it shows all
   letters backward,
If you try it
   with this book.
(Just hold this book
   up to a mirror).

mix

Gyro is cooking for a group;
He's mixing things to make a soup.

money

Coins and paper for buying things—
It goes fast, it must have wings.
This old Egyptian has a smile;
He found some money beside the Nile.

monkey

This animal's great
at climbing trees
And leaps among them
with the greatest of ease.

month

One lasts about four weeks, my dear.
It takes twelve months to make a year.

moon

Stars often fill
   the sky at night,
But the moon is
   the boldest sight,
And it gives off
   the greatest light.

morning

It's the time of day
   from dawn till noon;
When I go to bed late,
   it comes too soon.

mother

A woman who
   has a family
Of sons and daughters
   like you and me.

mountain

A mountain is a very
   high hill.
They started at noon and
   they're climbing still.

mouse

The tiny thing is mostly tail;
It's not our favorite animal.
Look out for this sharp-toothed little mouse.
It'll chew holes throughout your house.

movie

Filmed pictures that move on a screen.
Some make you laugh, some make you scream.

mud
When you mix water
and earth, I guess,
You're bound to get
a soggy mess.

music
Sounds that are made
in a special way
In pretty tunes that
you sing or play.

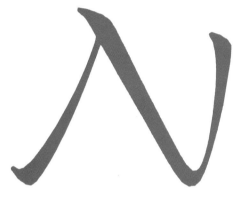

nail
Sharp pieces of metal,
thin and hard,
To fix a wood fence
in the backyard.

narrow
Spaghetti is something you have tried;
It comes in sizes from thin to wide.

naughty
When you're not doing what you should.
It means that you're not being good.

needle
Take a lesson from
  young Mother Crow—
Use this thin piece of
  metal when you sew.

neighbor
This is someone who lives nearby.
When new ones come I always try
To get a look at the family
To see if they have kids like me.

nest
It doesn't have a street address,
It has no door, I must confess,
It has no cellar nor a dome,
But the bird is glad to call it home.

new
Something just made,
  something bold,
Because it's different
  from the old.

nice
Someone friendly,
  someone kind:
I sort of had
  you in my mind.

night
The darkest part of the day,
When light and sunshine go away.

noise

To hear different sounds
   is one of our joys.
But if sound is too loud,
   it really annoys.

number

This word tells
   how many you see.
Is it one, or two,
   or three?

nut

A seed or fruit with
   a hard shell.
If one hits you,
   you sure can tell.

nurse

The doctor has so much to do,
The nurse helps him to help you, too.
The picture shows you what we mean.
The nurse is scrubbing the doctor clean.

ocean

A saltwater sea bigger
   than the land,
Walk near it and get
   your shoes full of sand.

old
This means alive a
  long, long time.
Here's an old fish
  that still is doing fine.

onion
This vegetable is
  easy to tell—
It has a very sharp,
  strong smell.

open
If we find a door that's shut,
We cannot get through it. But
If the door is opened wide,
It is easy to walk inside.

orange
Eat it or drink it;
  either way,
Have this sweet
  fruit every day.

oven
The part of a stove
  where you can bake
Vegetables and
  meat and cake.

owl
It has a curved beak
  and huge eyes.
Nighttime is when
  this wise bird flies.

pail
The cook gave Goofy
  a quarter
To bring him some
  pails of water;
They were heavy
  buckets he got,
But they had handles
  that helped a lot.

paint

A fish whose name
  was Muller
Decided to change
  his color.
He was in such
  an awful rush,
That he used liquid
  color and a brush
And said, "I sure
  used to be duller."

pancake

With a frying pan
  you can make
This delicious thin,
  round cake.
There is no tastier
  breakfast than
Pancakes with
  syrup or jam.

paper

The stuff on which we print or write,
Or wrap a package in, nice and tight.

parrot

A bright-colored bird with a big beak.
You can teach the parrot how to speak.
You may take the parrot for some walks,
But it might cause trouble when it talks!

party

When a lot of people
  decide to come
Together somewhere
  to have fun.

passenger

A person who rides
  in a plane or bus;
But the car is used
  by most of us.

pay

Money you give for
    things you buy;
Sometimes it seems
    they're priced too high.
But when the circus
    comes to town,
We can't wait to
    put our money down.

pea

One of the vegetables for our needs,
A pod full of pretty round green seeds.
Split the pod and out they fall,
Each a perfect round green ball.

peace

A happy time, when things are right,
And no one gets into a fight.

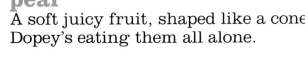

pear

A soft juicy fruit, shaped like a cone.
Dopey's eating them all alone.

pen

It's an ink-filled
    writing tool
That you can use
    at home or school.

pencil

A piece of wood,
    hey-diddle-diddle,
With a black lead
    in the middle.
And if you think
    black is a bore,
You'll find other
    colors in the store.

people
Women, boys, girls, and men—
This word means all of them.

pet
A tame animal
  we keep at home.
The wild ones live
  outside and roam.

photograph
Boy, oh, boy! Do I have fun,
Taking pictures of everyone
With the camera my folks left for me,
Last year under the Christmas tree.

piano
A very large music box,
  if you please,
That makes musical sounds
  when you hit the keys.

picnic
When you take food outdoors to eat,
Pack sandwiches and something sweet.

picture
Any photo, drawing,
  or painting you make.
You should keep them
  all for old times' sake.
If you hang them
  on the wall,
Please be careful
  they don't fall.

pie

Fruit cooked in pastry, what a sight!
Donald can't wait to take a bite.
You'll burn your tongue—don't be a fool!
Wait awhile and the pie will cool.

pig

This fat farm animal with curly tail
Will eat garbage from a pail.
One thing I thought I'd never see
Was a fat pig eating in a tree!

pillow

A bag filled with feathers, or something soft,
To put your head on when you're dozing off.
This special night Goofy is
Sleeping on gift packages.

pin

A piece of metal
    pointed and thin,
It holds things together
    when its point goes in.

pink

A pretty color
    nice and bright
You get if you mix
    red with white.

planet

A star in the sky
    on a regular run
That moves in a circle
    around the sun.

plant

Things with leaves
    and flowers grow
Out of the ground
    from roots below.
Scrooge is silly
    as silly can be.
He's trying to grow
    a money tree.

plum

A tasty fruit you
    may have tried,
And found a large
    hard pit inside.

pocket

To carry things, everyone knows,
You need these bags sewn into your clothes.

poem

A piece of writing
    you might pick.
It's like a song
    without music.

pond

A small lake where these ducks can swim.
They're about to welcome Junior in.

pony

A small horse is called a pony.
Big Bad Pete is riding Tony.

postcard

A thin piece of cardboard
   you can send
Through the mail to
   a good friend.

post office

Every one of us should know
It's where your letters come and go.
Postcards, too, pass in and out,
And packages, without a doubt.

pot

A deep bowl used to
   cook food hot;
In the kitchen
   there are a lot.

potato

A common vegetable that's found
Growing underneath the ground.

pour

To use water from a can,
Tilt it forward, my good man!
Goofy waters every hour.
It's his very first spring flower.

pretend

You can do real things
   with anyone,
But make-believe
   is also fun.
Here is something you've
   never seen—
Clarabelle acting
   as a queen.

puppet
A doll moved by a
    hand inside,
Or one to which long
    strings are tied.

puppy
A young dog is
    cuddly and cute;
This one's learning
    to salute.

queen
A woman who rules a whole country.
This card was caught painting her tree.

question
It seems no matter
    where you go
There is something
    someone wants to know.

quilt
A thick, padded,
    warm bedcover.
I have one I got
    from Mother.

quiet
Not speaking or making any noise
Is hard for little girls and boys.

rabbit
A long-eared animal
  you can get
That makes a cute
  and furry pet.

rain
Goofy sits with his head bowed,
As drops of water fall from a cloud.
They are only tiny drops, and yet
They're quite enough to get him wet.

rainbow
A sight in the sky
  now and again,
Where the sun shines
  through the rain.
It forms an arch of
  pretty colors.
The sight is worth
  a million dollars.

rat
This animal is no friend of man.
It will eat our food if it can.
It lives in buildings, fields, or trees,
And very often spreads disease.

rattle

It's the noise you
hear whenever
You shake some hard
things together.

read

To understand the
printed word,
Whether you're man,
mouse, or bird.

red

A stoplight is a common sight;
To make us stop, the color is bright.

refrigerator

A cold box to hold
the food we eat;
It keeps food fresh,
keeps out the heat.

reindeer

A kind of deer that
runs and races
In some of the world's
coldest places.

restaurant

A place that serves
food down the street
Where you have to
pay to eat.

66

ride

A car carries
   you inside,
An animal carries
   you on the outside.

river

Water that flows from the
   hills to the sea.
If it ever ran backward,
   where would we be?

road

Outside the city, a
   long wide street,
Where cars move so fast
   they're hard to beat.

rock

A large piece of stone that may
Lie still for many a night and day.
But if it rolls, get out of the way!

rocketship

A special machine, with
   an engine so strong
It can shoot into space
   and take people along.

roof

A house without one
   would be a shame.
It's the cover on top
   that keeps out the rain.

room

A house is divided
into spaces,
All of them are
special places,
Some are for sleep,
some are for fun;
Mickey's is a
messy one.

root

Part of a plant that grows underground.
Some make good food and are sold by the pound.

rope

Strong and thick, it's
like a string
That will tie
most anything.

round

A circle, a ball,
the letter O,
All are as round
as a zero.

rubber

Something that will
bounce or stretch,
A thin band or a
ball to catch.

ruler

This is a straight piece
of metal or wood
That helps you draw
a line real good.

run

When he is moving
   fast, you see,
His legs are
   traveling quickly.

sad

When you break the
   best toy you had,
You're not happy.
   You are sad.

same

These two bad guys
   are dressed the same.
There's no difference
   you can name.

sand

Small grains of rock that you may see
In great amounts beside the sea.

sandwich

Just watch him make lunch,
You'll see what we mean;
It's two pieces of bread
With food in between.

scarf

Here's a happy
   traveling goose
With his cloth neckpiece
   flying loose.

school

Where we learn to read and write.
Teachers help us do it right.

scientist

You won't catch the
   scientist napping;
He's finding out why
   things are happening.

scissors

Two blades screwed together
   will cut anything,
Like thread or cloth,
   or a piece of string.

secret

Wherever you go,
  this also goes.
It's something no
  other person knows.

seesaw

A long board for up and down rides,
Fastened at the center, equal on both sides.
Then sit on one end, my little friend,
And get someone else on the other end.

sew

One cloth is yellow,
  the other is red,
Held together with
  needle and thread.

share

You do this when
You give part of something to a friend.
If you have a soda, you might think
To offer someone else a drink.

sharp

An edge that can cut
  celery in a bowl,
Or a pointed thing
  that makes a hole.

shelf
A board that you
fasten to a wall;
It can hold most
anything at all.

shell
It's a hard cover
you may find
On animals of
many kinds,
Like insects, clams,
and turtles, but
Don't forget the
egg and nut.

ship
I guess we all would
like to be
On those large boats
that cross the sea.

shoes
Goofy wears these to cover his feet.
An umbrella keeps off the sun's heat.

shop
A place to
buy all sorts of things,
Like clothing, books, and
waterwings.

shout
When somebody speaks very loud,
Then earplugs ought to be allowed.

shovel

A tool for digging
in the ground.
It's nice when extra
help is found.

shy

When you are shy, it's not a joke.
You're not at ease with other folk.

silly

Being silly is fun for some,
But it's not clever. It looks dumb.

sing

To make music with your voice;
What you sing is your own choice.

sink

In any house you'll
come across it:
It is a bowl
with a water faucet.

sister

A sister is a female who
Has the same parents as you do.

sit

This is a position
  we all have tried:
Shift your weight to
  your backside.
You stand to open
  the door for me,
You sit when you read
  or watch TV.

skeleton

You couldn't stand
or run or ride
Without these bones
you have inside.

skirt

A piece of cloth to suit your taste
Which wraps around you from your waist.

sled

This platform with runners
  of steel will go
When the ground is all covered
  with ice and with snow.

sleep

It's the time you're not awake.
Sleep comes even to a snake.

slip

Something not on
    purpose tried,
A slip is an accidental
    slide.

slow

It's when you're not moving fast,
And let other things go past.

small

The little mouse is having fun
Playing on the great big drum.

smell

We use the nose—hers or his—
To tell us just what something is.
Sometimes we sniff and we can tell
What it is by its special smell.

smile

When you are happy to see friends,
Turn your mouth up at the ends.

75

snore
Sometimes in sleep,
  you girls and boys
Make a very loud
  breathing noise.

snow
Drops of water in the sky
Are frozen, and that is why
They fall to earth as snow nearby.
You can pile it up wherever it falls,
And roll it into big snowballs.

sock
A baglike covering
  that you use
To put on your feet
  before the shoes.

soft
Goofy was napping in the yard,
But he thought the ground was hard.
So he tried a couch, soft and deep,
And there he quickly fell asleep.

somersault
Do you know how
  good it feels
To put yourself head
  over heels?

76

son

If you're a son then
you must be
A boy in somebody's
family.

song

Words and music
played together,
Some songs will go
on forever.

space

Way up high
in the empty sky,
Higher than
our planes can fly,
So far away there
is no air;
Just rocketships
can go up there.

spoon

When you're in the kitchen take a look—
It's a tool we use when we eat and cook.

spot

A little mark you can see some place;
It could be a freckle on your face.

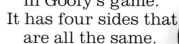

square
Look at the blue square
in Goofy's game.
It has four sides that
are all the same.

stairs
Sets of steps you
walk up or down.
As usual, Goofy plays
the clown.

stamp
A little piece of
paper that
Has a colored front,
with glue on the back;
On your package
or your mail,
It gets delivery
without fail.

stars
The stars and moon
shine bright at night.
They help you to see
by their light.

start
To start means to begin somewhere;
If you don't start, you get nowhere.
This little boy will do just fine,
He's just starting to paint a sign.

step
You put one foot
before the other,
Walking to school with
your big brother.

stick

How would you use this piece of wood?
It is too thin to be much good.
The bird would like it for her nest.
Little Pig thinks a fireplace best.

sting

Some insects have
   a sharp part, too;
It hurts if it gets
   stuck in you.

stone

A small piece of rock is a stone;
Many, many kinds are known.

stop

To finish whatever
   one is doing:
When cows get fed,
   they stop their mooing.

story

An adventure in a book that's read,
Or one that's told to us in bed.

straight

Not curved or
   crooked anywhere,
It goes direct from
   here to there.

79

straw
Dry, yellow grass
   that farmers keep
On which the animals
   can sleep.

street
A road where motorcars
   can ride
To get to houses
   on each side.

string
A piece of thread that's
   long enough
To tie up every
   kind of stuff.

strong
Able to carry heavy things,
Or wrestle and fight in boxing rings.

submarine
Little Mary's teacher taught her
That this ship moved under water;
Thinking of the deepest sea,
Mary said, "That's not for me!"

sun
The sun is such a
   splendid sight.
It gives us all its
   warmth and light.

supermarket

This shop sells food
   that's fit for kings,
And many, many
   other things.
You help yourself,
   I do believe,
And pay your bill
   before you leave.

WATCH IT, BUDDY!

sweep

I brush the dirt off of the floor,
But by next day, there's always more.

table

A flat-topped piece
   of furniture,
With legs to raise
   it off the floor.

talk

It can be something said by you,
Or something said by others, too.

tall

Something very high
That seems to point up to the sky.

T t

taxi

A car ride where
   you pay a fare;
Most of the time
   it gets you there.

teacher

Some are women,
  some are men:
You learn a lot of
  things from them.

tears
Now and then everyone cries
With drops of water from their eyes.

teeth
White bones in your mouth you use to bite;
Brush them each day to keep them bright.

telephone
A machine that you talk into night or day;
Folks hear your voice from miles away.

television
A machine that you
  watch every day
For pictures and sounds
  from far away.

tent
To sleep outdoors
  you need to fix
This heavy cloth with
  rope and sticks.

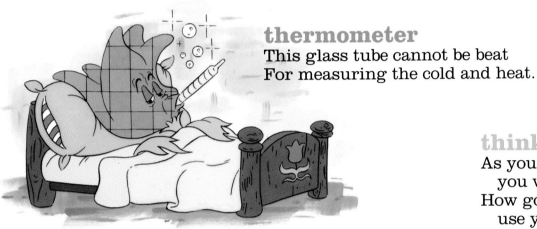

thermometer
This glass tube cannot be beat
For measuring the cold and heat.

think
As you get older
  you will find
How good it is to
  use your mind.

throw
A very hard push
  into the air,
Like what they're doing with
  the beehive there.

ticket
A piece of paper that you buy
To ride a bus or train or to fly.
You can get your tickets, too,
For the circus or the zoo.

tiny
This is very very small,
Something we hardly see at all.

toast

We brown our bread
   by using heat
If we like it hot
   and crisp to eat.

together

To be with something
   or someone,
Like Tweedledee
   and Tweedledum.

tomato

A small red fruit that's
   smooth and round.
The supermarket's
   where they're found;
You can buy them
   by the pound.

tool

It helps us to get
   something made:
(A wrench or hammer
   or a spade).

top

The highest point that there can be,
Like the top of a hill or of a tree.
It's also a small spinning toy
That's fun for a little girl or boy.

town

A place that we will find wherever
They build houses close together.

toy

For most kids it's
a special joy.
Even King Tut had
a stuffed toy.

tractor

A machine with great big
wheels and springs
That's made to pull
real heavy things.

train

Through the hail and sleet and rain,
Nothing stops the speeding train.
Thanks to miles of railroad track,
It gets there, and it gets back.

tree

Trees have branches
and a trunk,
Trees have got a
lot of spunk;
They suffer heat and
snow and rain,
And grow new leaves
in Spring again.

triangle

Our dictionary here defines
It as a shape made of three straight lines.

trick

Clever things that
   people do
To give fun to folks
   like me and you.
Some do flips dressed
   like a clown,
Some fly an airplane
   upside down.

truck

You see them everywhere
   on roads:
Big cars that carry
   heavy loads.

trumpet

You blow into the
   mouthpiece, then
Loud music comes out the
   other end.

tunnel

Sometimes, in order
   to get somewhere,
We dig a hole to get
   us there.
It could be a hole
   cut through a mound,
Or a hole that is
   dug underground.

turkey

A large bird with
   wings so small
That it can hardly
   fly at all.
Most of them are
   bred that way,
To make big meals
   on the holiday.

turtle

He lives in the water very well,
Protected by his big hard shell.

U u

umbrella

A cloth spread over
   metal ribs, but,
If the weather's dry,
   you keep it shut.
If it's raining,
   then instead
You open it above
   your head.

valentine

A card to someone that will say,
"All my love on Valentine's Day."

van

It's not a truck or
   passenger car,
But it can travel
   fast and far,
Working at a steady
   pace,
Carrying things
   from place to place.

vegetable

A kind of plant that we are able
To cook, and eat at the dining table.

violet

A small flower, purple and white.
Growing wild, it's a pretty sight.

violin
Move a bow across its strings,
And, oh! what joy its music brings.

wagon
An open four-wheeled cart;
It makes a bumpy stop and start.

THE DOCTOR IS **IN**

wait
To stay somewhere, just in case
Someone comes or something takes place.

walk
To move your feet from place to place,
Going along at a normal pace.

wall
Something built of brick or stone,
Like the side of a barn or of a home,
Or a kind of fence that stands alone.

warm

Warm is not hot,
  so I've been told,
But it's more hot
  than it is cold.

wash

It won't make you nice,
It won't make you mean.
One thing it will do—
It will make you clean.

watch

This small clock worn
  on the wrist
Is a good graduation
  gift.

water

A liquid that is everywhere,
In lakes and seas—even in the air.

weak

Someone or something that's not strong.
We try to fix the thing that's wrong.

weather

What kind of tomorrow
   will we get?
Hot or cold,
   dry or wet?

week

Seven days
   equal a week
To work and play and
   eat and sleep.

weight

Little Hiawatha
   can't relax,
He's lifting a
   heavy battle-ax;
It seems heavier
   on some days.
(A scale could tell
   him what it weighs.)

wet

Goofy is giving the water a try.
He is wet, no longer dry.
He might meet a seabird or squid,
Swimming around in this liquid.

whale

The largest animals
   in the sea,
They mean a lot
   to you and me.
Fishermen should
   let them be.

wheel

These are for bike,
  bus, and car.
Without them they
  won't get too far.
Flat circles that roll
  things right along;
Any other shape would
  sure be wrong.

whisper

To speak in a very low voice
Is a matter of your own choice.
There are times it's quite all right,
But other times it's impolite.
At its worst or at its best,
It gives your vocal cords a rest.

whistle

Blow through your lips,
  closed and round,
And make this high,
  melodic sound.

white

You're quite right—some
  gulls are white.
So is the paper on which
  you write.

wide

When the river rises
  at high tide,
It is a long way
  from side to side.

wild

Some things we nurse
with food and fuss,
But wild things do as
well without us.

window

The opening in a building wall
That lets in light and air for all.

witch

She is believed to do magical things;
She flies with a broom instead of with wings.

wolf

A dangerous animal
in the wild,
which will attack a
man or child.

woman

She can do things on her own.
She is a female, fully grown.

wood

To get it we cut tall trees down
So we can build houses in a town,
And fences, floors, and furniture;
All things we must have, I am sure.

word

It's a sound we
can understand,
We learn to write it
out by hand.

work

The effort folks make
to get things done;
It's not play, yet
it can be fun.

world

The earth and all persons
far and near,
As well as the animals and
atmosphere.

write

In order to do this,
you must succeed
In drawing letters
and words that folks can read.

wrong

This is not right,
it's just not done,
Like stealing supper
from someone.

93

x-ray
A special photograph
  that tries
To show a picture
  of your insides.

ACME X-RAY

year
Next year, will you feel bolder
When you will be one year older?
On your birthday you can say,
"A year is just twelve months away."

yell
There are times when
  we have no choice
But to call out in a
  loud voice.

yellow
A bright color that
  you know;
Bananas and lemons
  have that sunny glow.

young
What we are early
  in life, we're told,
When we are not
  considered old.

94

zebra

A small horse dressed
  like a clown,
With dark stripes
  running up and down.

zero

Zero doesn't mean
  big or small;
Zero means nothing
  at all.

zigzag

When you're running, have you tried
Moving quickly from side to side?
If you have, you've done just fine,
Making a crooked zigzag line.

zipper

A fastener that will hold together
Two pieces of fabric or of leather,
And release them quickly, too,
If that is what you want to do.

zoo

Wild animals living in a cage or pen,
Where people can come and look at them.